Donated by:
Sandi Rowe

LIFE IN A
GREEK
TRADING
PORT

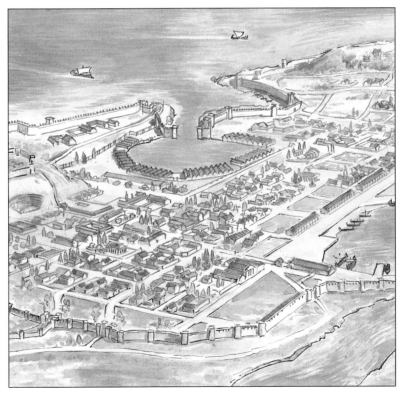

JANE SHUTER

Heinemann Library
Chicago, Illinois

Customer Service 888-454-2279
Visit our website at www.heinemann classroom.com

Originated by Modern Age
Printed in China by WKT Company Limited

09 08 07 06 05
10 9 8 7 6 5 4 3 2 1

Library of Congress Cataloging-in-Publication Data

Shuter, Jane.
  Life in a Greek trading port / Jane Shuter.
      p. cm. -- (Picture the past)
  Includes bibliographical references and index.
  ISBN 1-4034-6444-8 (hc) -- ISBN 1-4034-6451-0 (pb)
  1. Harbors--Greece--History--To 1500--Juvenile literature. 2.
Greece--Commerce--History--To 1500--Juvenile literature. 3. Greece--Social
life and customs--Juvenile literature. I. Title. II. Series.
  DF107.S58 2004
  387.1'0938--dc22
                                    2004025844

Acknowledgments:
The publishers would like to thank the following for permission to reproduce photographs:AKG p. **15** (Archives CDA/Guillo), **18** (Erich Lessing), **21** (John Hios), **24**; Angence Photographique de la Réunion des Musées Nationaux p. **8**; Art Archive pp. **9**, (Musée d'Archeologies Mediterranéene, Marseilles/Dagli Orti,), **23** (Musée du Louvre, Paris/Dagli Orti); Bridgeman p. **13** (British Museum), **25**; British Museum p. **20**, **29** (Werner Forman); Corbis p. **6**; Scala pp. **10** (Ministero Beni e Attivita Culturali), **14** (Foto Scala, Florence), **16**; Staaliche Museen, Berlin p. **26**; Werner Forman pp. **12**, **17**, **28** (Museo Archelogico Siracusa).

Cover photograph of a bowl showing an ancient Greek ship reproduced with permission of AKG/Erich Lessing.

Every effort has been made to contact copyright holders of any material reproduced in this book. Any omissions will be rectified in subsequent printings if notice is given to the publishers.

The paper used to print this book comes from sustainable resources.

Any words appearing in bold, **like this**, are explained in the Glossary.

Contents

Who Were the
Ancient Greeks? 4

A Safe Harbor 6

How Ships Were Built 8

Where Ships Sailed 10

Sailors 12

Traders 14

Warehouses and Docks 16

Warships 18

Pirates and Explorers 20

Family Life 22

Traveling 24

Food and Drink 26

Free Time 28

Glossary 30

Further Reading 31

Index 32

Who Were the Ancient Greeks?

Much of Greece is covered by mountains. This made it hard to travel around by land in ancient times. But Greece also has sea on three sides, in which there are many islands. So the sea was always important to the ancient Greeks. They traveled by sea as much as they could. This meant they needed **harbors** to land in. Some of these harbors grew into **ports**—places where ships came from all over ancient Greece. Ports were especially useful to **traders**, because they could meet there to exchange goods.

Look for these:
The ship shows you the subject of each chapter. The picture of an amphora, or Greek vase, shows you boxes with interesting facts, figures, and quotes about life in a Greek port.

TIMELINE OF EVENTS IN THIS BOOK

800 B.C. First **city states**; warships have developed metal rams at the front

776 B.C. First Olympic Games

490-467 B.C. War with Persia

480 B.C. Sea battle of Salamis

546 B.C. First Persian attacks on Greece

462 B.C. Democracy in Athens

461–451 B.C. Athens and Sparta at war

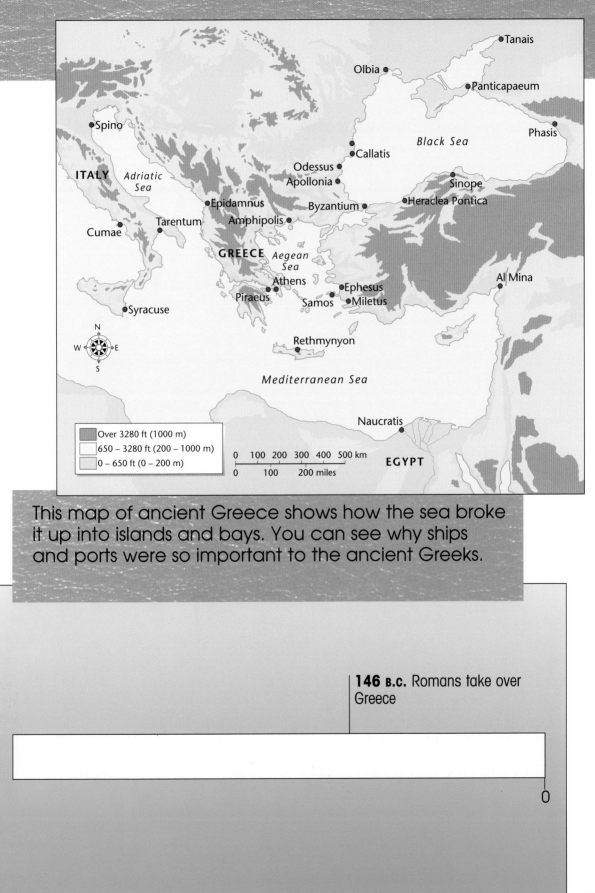

This map of ancient Greece shows how the sea broke it up into islands and bays. You can see why ships and ports were so important to the ancient Greeks.

146 B.C. Romans take over Greece

0

A Safe Harbor

All ships needed a safe **harbor**—a place on the coast to keep them safe at night or in bad weather. Fishermen and their families lived in villages by harbors. Some harbors grew into busy **ports**. They had to be big enough to hold a lot of ships and be in easy reach of cities and other ports. Sailors, **traders**, and their families lived and worked there. Other people came there to buy or exchange **goods**.

PIRAEUS

Piraeus was probably one of the first places used as a safe harbor for Athens. From 493 B.C. on it grew into a port with its own **warehouses** and **docks**. Later, it became a bigger town with a theater and **temples**. The road from Piraeus to Athens had high walls on each side to make it safe.

Even today, many Greek islands can only be reached by sea. A safe harbour is still important.

6

here was a third harbor
or fighting ships just a little
vay along the coast.

These sheds were used
to store and repair
fighting ships.

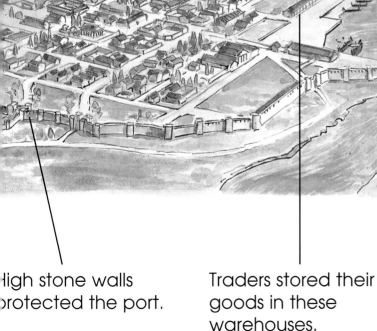

High stone walls
protected the port.

Traders stored their
goods in these
warehouses.

This harbor was used
by trading ships
and fighting ships.

How Ships Were Built

Shipbuilders made ships of different sizes and shapes, depending on what they were used for. Warships were long, to carry lots of people. They were light and low, to move quickly through the water. They had oars, for rowing the ship when there was no wind. **Trade** ships did not need to be fast. They simply had to hold a lot of **cargo**. So they had high sides and fewer oars.

These are some of the kinds of simple wooden tools a ship's carpenter would have used.

8

Shipmakers shaped the **keel** first. This was the long, thick piece of wood that ran along the bottom of the ship, in the center. They made the outside frame by joining planks of wood tightly together, joined to the keel. Once the outside was finished, shipbuilders nailed planks across the inside to strengthen it. They painted the outside with **tar** to make it waterproof.

Many ships had a sail for using the wind to move forward. The sail hung from a mast in the middle of the ship.

Where Ships Sailed

The ancient Greeks knew that the sea was full of dangers. Ships had to face storms and **pirates**. If bad weather blew them out to sea, they might get lost because they had no proper maps or instruments to help them **navigate**. But the ancient Greeks wanted to **trade** and to set up **colonies**—settlements of Greeks in other lands. So they went to sea despite the dangers.

This map shows how the Greek **city states** set up colonies around the coast of the Mediterranean Sea and the Black Sea. They traded in all these places and got there by following the line of the coast.

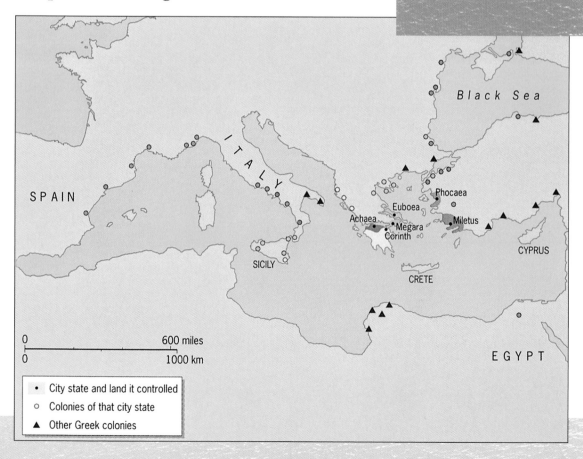

Black Sea

ITALY

SPAIN

Phocaea
Euboea
Achaea
Megara
Corinth
Miletus

CYPRUS

SICILY

CRETE

EGYPT

	600 miles
0	
0	1000 km

- City state and land it controlled
- Colonies of that city state
- ▲ Other Greek colonies

To navigate, sailors tried to keep land in sight at all times. This is why they traveled mainly by daylight and landed at night. Some sailors traveled to the same places a lot, so they knew the shape of the land and how long it took to get to places. At other times, sailors asked in **ports** until they found someone who could tell give them directions.

This lion-shaped make-up pot was found in Greece. It comes from the other side of the Mediterranean, near North Africa. It shows us that the ancient Greeks must have sailed there.

SAILING FARTHER

One Greek traveler, Pythias, got as far as Great Britain and wrote about his experiences there. But Greek ships did not sail all the way to Britain. Historians think he got there by sailing to southern Spain in a Greek ship. After getting to Spain, he probably got a ride on another ship.

Sailors

There were not many full-time sailors. **Citizens** of the **city state** rowed and fought on warships. Ships that went exploring or to **trade** often had some **experienced** sailors on board. Rich traders could hire an experienced captain and crew to sail their ships, but this cost a lot. New traders sometimes bought a ship with friends. Often, these traders sailed their ships themselves.

Stories of the dangers sailors faced told of storms and **pirates**. They also talked about imaginary creatures sent by the gods. The **sirens** on this vase sang to make sailors sail their ships on to rocks, wrecking them.

Sailors did not spend all their time at sea. Spring and summer, when the weather was better, were the best times for sailing. So sailors often had a second job to do when they were not at sea. If they lived in a **port**, their job was often to do with ships or fishing. They could make ropes, sails or nets, or build and repair boats.

This vase painting shows young men diving for natural sponges that grew on the sea bed.

Traders

Some people in **trade** sold just one thing, such as **grain**. Other traders sold a mix of different things. They chose the **goods** they thought would make them the most money. Wine, oil, and grain were traded most often. A ship sunk near Cyprus in about 350 B.C. was carrying 404 jars of wine, about 10,000 almonds in sacks and 29 millstones to use for grinding corn.

This vase shows a man buying fish from a fishmonger. There were no refrigerators or freezers in ancient Greece, so fish was sold the day it was caught.

Many traders borrowed money to buy goods to trade. They hoped to make enough money to pay back the borrowed money and the amount the **banker** charged for lending it and still have some money left over. The banker sometimes agreed not to ask for the money back if the ship sank.

A TRADER'S TRICK

A trader called Hegestratos borrowed money to buy grain to trade. He did not buy grain, but kept the money and sailed the ship away empty. He made a hole in the ship to sink it. His banker would not ask for the money back if the ship sank. But when Hegestratos jumped overboard, he could not find his escape boat. He drowned. The sailors mended the hole and got the ship home, and the trick was discovered.

Each Greek **city state** had different coins. The countries outside Greece also had different coins. So Greek traders needed to work with bankers who could swap different kinds of coins.

Warehouses and Docks

Ports needed space in the **harbor** for ships to land and **warehouses** near the **docks**, so **traders** could store their **goods**. A large port, like Piraeus, often had two docks. There was a dock with large sheds for storing warships. There was a bigger dock for trade ships. This did not have ship sheds, but it had warehouses all around it.

SHIP SHEDS

The **city state** of Athens had hundreds of warships, which were kept in sheds so that they stayed dry and could be repaired easily. The sheds had a stone ramp sloping down into the water for each ship. **Slaves** or donkeys pulled the ships up and down these ramps on ropes.

Warehouses were locked and guarded against thieves. Traders who bought and sold really precious goods, like this gold jewelry, often stored them at home, not at the docks.

Most traders had several slaves working at their warehouse, loading and unloading. Unlike many Greek buildings, warehouses had solid walls on all sides and no windows. They had to keep the goods inside dry and also keep out thieves and animals. If mice or rats got into a **grain** warehouse, they could eat and quickly spoil all the grain inside.

Traders could sell Greek marble and stone statues for a lot of money. But the statues were hard to move and heavy to carry by boat. If a statue was dropped during loading, it could make a hole that would sink the ship.

Warships

The first Greek warships sailed close enough to each other for those on board to fight using their hands. By 800 B.C., the Greeks were using a ram—a heavy lump of metal on the front of the ship. They sailed at the enemy ships, hoping to make holes in the sides of them that would be big enough to sink the ship. Over time, the Greeks built their ships with two, then three, levels of rowers to make them faster and quicker at escaping the enemy. The ships must have been very crowded.

This vase painting shows an early warship, with just one row of oars on each side.

In 480 B.C., the Persians invaded Greece and won several land battles. Their army and **navy** headed for Athens. The Athenian navy trapped the Persians and beat them. A Greek playwright wrote a Persian view of the battle: "The Greeks made a circle around us and rammed holes in our ships. You could not see the water, it was so full of wrecked ships and dead men."

This is a modern artist's idea of how the Greek ships moved toward the trapped Persian ships during the 480 B.C. invasion.

Pirates and Explorers

Usually people went to sea to fish, to **trade**, or to fight. But some people went to sea as **pirates** or explorers. Pirates usually lived and worked from an island not too far from the coast. Pirates had their own rules. They did not usually rob ships from their own **city state**. They robbed trading ships and pirates from other city states.

This vase painting shows a pirate ship attacking a trade ship. The pirate ship, on the right, was designed like a warship. You can see the ram on the front, getting closer to the trading ship.

HOME AGAIN

Alexander had thought that Nearchus and his men were dead. He was surprised to see them back. They were sunburned and tired. One Greek historian wrote, "Their hair was long and tangled. Their bodies were thin and dirty." But they were alive.

Ancient Greek sailors believed Poseidon, the god of the sea, could send them calm seas or storms.

The ancient Greeks who went exploring were usually sent by the leaders of their city state. The most famous Greek explorer was called Nearchus. Alexander the Great, the first person to rule all of Greece, sent him exploring in 325 B.C. Nearchus took about 100 ships and explored the Indian Ocean for about a year. His sailors, who were used to the calmer Mediterranean Sea, were terrified by the waves and got very seasick.

Family Life

Sailors and their families usually lived in **port** cities. They lived like other Greeks of their time. Women stayed at home while men went to work. Greek women were usually expected to stay indoors most of the time, while their husbands did the shopping. But sailors' wives were left alone when their husbands went to sea. So, in ports, women sent a **slave** to shop, or shopped in a group.

While their husbands were gone, women did the same duties they did when their husbands were home. They spun wool, wove cloth, and brought up the children. This woman is making a funeral wreath.

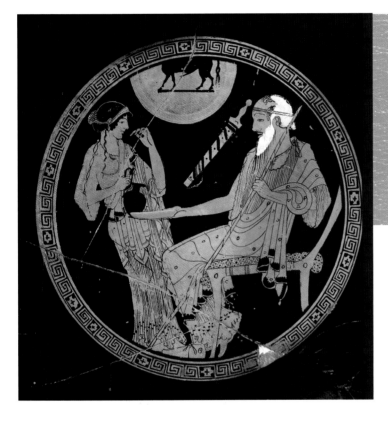

Most ancient Greeks had at least one slave to do housework and serve meals. Men and women did not eat together.

Rich **traders** often did not live in the port. They lived in the city. Slaves ran their businesses for them, although the traders visited from time to time to check on things. Poorer traders lived in the port but did not always sail on trading trips. They did not leave their families for long periods of time.

SLAVES

A man who could afford to keep a slave but did not was looked down upon. This was the kind of person this Greek writer laughs at: "When he shops, he carries the meat from the market himself, in his hands, and the vegetables in the fold of his cloak. He stays indoors when his clothes are at the laundry [because he is too mean to buy a change of clothes]."

Ships were used for fighting and **trading**, but they also carried passengers. Ancient Greeks did not travel, either on foot or by boat, unless they had to. They might travel to see a sick relative, or to go to a **religious festival**. They traveled short distances in local fishing boats. For longer distances, they had to find a trade ship going in the right direction.

This vase shows the god Dionysus asleep on the deck of a ship. Sleeping on deck was uncomfortable, but sleeping below the deck, where the **goods** were stored, was both uncomfortable and airless.

Travelers got to the nearest **port** on foot, on a cart, or riding a donkey. This depended on how far they had to go and how rich they were. All travel was dirty, dangerous, and uncomfortable. On ships, travelers and sailors slept on deck if they could not land at night. If they could land at night, they slept on the beach.

WHERE TO STAY

Travelers could not always leave the port as soon as they arrived. They had to find a ship going in the right direction. If they could, people stayed with family or friends. If not, they stayed at an **inn**. This gave them a bed for the night. But travelers at the time complained that most inns were not comfortable or clean.

Ancient Greeks often wanted to know if they would come back safely from a journey. This soldier is looking at the insides of a bird he has sacrificed to the gods. The Greeks believed this could tell the future.

Food and Drink

Ancient Greek sailors, fighters, and explorers ate and drank what they could, when they could. If they landed at night, they slept and cooked on the beach. Often they ate very little but the fish they caught, possibly with some herbs they found near the beach.

Sailors cooked directly over or in the fires they lit on the beach. The fires also helped to keep them warm at night.

Coriander Fish

The ancient Greeks ate much more fish than other kinds of meat. They grilled many fish whole, but sometimes they baked them in a pot on the fire, as they would have done for this recipe.

You will need:
2 fillets of white fish, such as halibut or cod
2 tablespoons of coriander seeds
1 teaspoon of salt
vegetable oil
some white wine vinegar

1 Heat the oven to 375°F (190°C).

2 Bake the coriander seeds on a baking sheet for 10 minutes. Leave them to cool. Put them with the salt in a plastic food bag and use a heavy rolling pin to crush them.

3 Put the fish in an oven dish that has been oiled with vegetable oil.

4 Sprinkle the salt and coriander mix over the fish.

5 Cover the dish with foil and bake in the oven for 20 minutes.

6 Remove from the oven and sprinkle vinegar over the fish.

Free Time

People who lived in Greek **ports** spent their free time in the same way as other ancient Greeks. The men spent most of their time outside, especially in the summer, when homes became too hot. They exercised, ate and drank, and gambled. Women spent their time together and with their children.

FUN AT SEA?

We know that many ancient Greeks thought sailing was dangerous. So they probably did not sail for pleasure, as people do today. We do know that they swam and fished for pleasure and exercise, especially men and boys.

These pottery animals, which appear to be a sheep, a rabbit, and a wild pig, were probably children's toys.

Babies and young children played with toys and with friends. But from the age of about seven, they had less and less free time. Girls helped their mothers around the house to learn how to run a home of their own. Boys either went to school or began to work with their father, learning his **trade**.

This terracotta statue shows Greek women playing a game called knucklebones. The game was played with cleaned animal bones, which is how it got its name.

Glossary

banker person who lends money to others in return for getting extra money back from them

bronze metal made by melting copper and tin together

cargo things taken by sea to be traded

citizen man who is born in a city to parents who are citizens there

city state city and the surrounding land it controls

colonies settlements in one country set up by people from another country

dock part of a harbor where ships can stay for long periods of time

experienced someone who has done something a lot and knows how to do it well

goods things that are made, bought, and sold

grain types of grasses with fat seeds that are eaten. Barley, wheat, rye, oats, and rice are all grains.

harbor sheltered place on the coast

inn houses where the owner rented out small rooms to people for the night. Some inns also served meals.

keel long, thick piece of wood that runs along the center of the ship's bottom

navigate to work out how to get from one place to another

navy ships used to fight for a country

pirates robbers that rob people at sea

ports where ships come to trade or land

religious festival several days of religious celebrations, usually held every year at the same time

sirens imaginary creatures with beautiful voices that sang to sailors to make them crash their ships against rocks and drown

slave person who is bought and sold by someone and has to work for that person

tar black sticky substance that is waterproof

temple place where gods and goddesses are worshiped

trade person's job; or the selling or swapping of goods

warehouse place where goods are stored

Further Reading

Books

Chrisp, Peter. *A Greek Theater*. Chicago: Raintree, 2001.

Hatt, Christine. *Ancient Greece*. Chicago: Heinemann Library, 2004.

Hicks, Peter. *Ancient Greece*. Chicago: Raintree, 2000.

Middleton, Haydn. *Ancient Greek Jobs*. Chicago: Heinemann Library, 2002.

Rees, Rosemary. *The Ancient Greeks*. Chicago: Heinemann Library, 1997.

Tames, Richard. *Ancient Greek Children*. Chicago: Heinemann Library, 2002.

Index

Alexander the
  Great 21
ancient Greece
  (map) 5
Athens 4, 6, 16, 19

bankers 15

canals 7
cargo 8
children 28, 29
citizens 12
city states 4, 10, 12,
  15, 16, 20, 21
coins 15
colonies 10

docks 6, 16

exploration 12, 21

family life 22–23
fish, baked 27
fishing boats 24
food and drink
  26–27
free time 28–29

games 29
goods 4, 6, 7, 14,
  16, 24
grain 14, 17

Great Britain 11

harbors 4, 6, 7, 16
Hesiod 13

inns 25

keels 9

navigation 10, 11
navy 19
Nearchus 21

Persians 4, 19
Piraeus 6, 16
pirates 10, 12, 20
ports 4, 6, 7, 11, 13,
  16–17, 22–23, 25,
  28
Pythias 11

religious festivals 24
repairing ships 13,
  16

sailors 6, 11, 12–13,
  15, 22, 25, 26
sails 9, 13
shipbuilding 8–9, 13
sirens 12
slaves 16, 17, 22, 23
statues 17, 29
storms 10, 12

tar 9
temples 6
thieves 16, 17
tools 8
toys 28
trade and traders
  4, 6, 7, 8, 10, 12,
  14–15, 16, 17, 20,
  23, 24, 29
trade ships 8, 12,
  14, 15, 16, 20, 24
travelers 24–25

vase paintings 12,
  13, 14, 18, 20, 22,
  23, 24, 25

warehouses 6, 7,
  16, 17
warships 4, 8, 12,
  16, 18–19, 20
winter 13
women 22, 23, 28,
  29